Dr. Seuss's

for Soprano, Boy Soprano, and Piano

Text by THEODOR GEISEL (Dr. Seuss)
Music by ROBERT KAPILOW

T0042531

Green Eggs and Ham

By Dr. Seuss

Edition Ed-3972
First Printing: December, 1995

G. SCHIRMER, Inc.

DISTRIBUTED BY

HAL•LEONARD
CORPORATION

7777 W. BLUEMOUND RD. P.O. BOX 13819 MILWAUKEE, WI 53213

PERFORMANCE NOTES
Audience Interactions

Although *Green Eggs and Ham* can be performed as a purely musical/theatrical event, I always precede the musical performance with an interactive session with the audience. I go out into the audience with a hand-held microphone and talk directly to the children and parents. (Kids love to hear themselves over a microphone!) This portion of the program ranges from 5 minutes to 30 minutes, depending on whether or not any other piece is programmed with *Green Eggs and Ham.* These sessions have turned out to be lots of fun and they greatly increase the audience's understanding of the performance.

Should the conductor wish to try one of these sessions, I would like to offer some suggestions based on what I have found to be successful.

I start from the premise that Dr. Seuss' story is a parable in which a child teaches an adult about prejudice—green eggs and ham representing all those things that we are sure we will not like even though we have not tried them. Consequently, I often begin by asking the children in the audience to tell me something they have gotten their parents to try that the parents were sure they would not like, for example, marshmallow fluff, or bungee jumping.

I then ask how they got their parents to try it. Did they whine? Threaten? Cajole? I have individual children stand and try different lines from *Green Eggs and Ham* using various intonations like whining, threatening, and so on. This gets them involved with listening to interpretation.

From this it is easy to move to musical issues. Since Sam–I–Am asks the Grouch to try the eggs over and over with no success, I ask the children what makes the final request successful? What would they do, if they were composers, to make the music of the last request special? Should it be the loudest, softest, longest, etc.? Then I suggest they listen closely, during the performance, to hear what I did to make this last request special and to tell me after the performance.

I often have the children pretend they are composers and do an interaction around the phrase "A train! A train! A train! A train! Could you, would you, could you, on a train?" First I ask them if they could imagine any sound or instrument associated with a train. Usually, someone thinks of a train whistle, and I show them how this whistle begins the phrase (m. 200). Then I ask if any melody

associated with a train comes to mind. Either someone thinks of "I've Been Working on the Railroad" or I play it, harmonized traditionally, and ask what it is. I proceed, bar by bar, to play the traditional harmonization followed by my "weird, modern" one. I even demonstrate how the "Dinah blow your horn" part or the "could you, would you, on a train" part becomes the lead-in to the next section. This heightens their awareness of the passage so they hear it when the piece is performed and brings them into the creative process of how a piece of music is written.

Another interaction that is both fun and instructive involves using the patter version of "I do not like them in a box." (m. 190). I teach the audience to say this phrase in rhythm until they have it memorized and can perform the whole unit as a group. This is also an opportunity to "rehearse" the audience like an orchestra and teach them about ensemble playing. I then have three or four children, who think they can perform the whole section, try it on stage. This can be uproariously funny and also amazing, as children can often perform it quite well. I then add pitch to the section and show them the shape, with hand gestures, how the melody moves in different ways—first down, then up, then sideways.

One final thing I do before every performance is to introduce each instrumentalist and have them play a short excerpt from the piece, to show the children something special to listen for. For example, the flutist might play the "in the dark" solo (m. 257) without flutter tonguing. I ask the children if they are scared. They answer no. Then the flutist plays it with flutter tonguing and I ask them which version is scarier. The trumpet player plays a solo with and without a mute, and so on.

These suggestions should convey the flavor of the type of interactive sessions I lead. No two are the same and new ideas constantly come up. The conductor may use some of the ideas I have found successful or develop his or her own ideas that will engage the audience.

I cannot recommend these sessions too strongly. They can often be as valuable as the performance of the piece itself and can create a wonderful opening for families into the magical, musical world of *Green Eggs and Ham.*

Suggested Staging

Green Eggs and Ham is intended as a concert piece and does not require a set or any elaborate props, but its effect is greatly enhanced by a theatrical kind of performance.

The soprano and child (which could be sung by a girl, interpreting the name as a nickname for Samantha) should establish a relationship (either neighbor/child, teacher/student, or whatever the performers make up) and interact theatrically. For example, they might enter separately (I often use m. 9 for Sam and m. 30 for the soprano) and create a scenario for the opening instrumental music. This could be a librarian reading prissily as a student interrupts her reading, or routines with "game-boys," backpacks, or anything else appropriate to the performers. The singers may also find ways to make use of instrumental passages between the sung/spoken sections and the cæsuras are used in some theatrical fashion.

Though the performers may create any staging scenario they wish, there are two moments that lend themselves to a particular staging. At m. 245 all the lights should go out except for the stand lights of the musicians. The entire "in the dark" section that follows is performed without lights until m. 281. During this section, the singers can use flashlights, matches, etc. to strobe the audience and bring this section to life. For example, the soprano could be afraid of the dark and be comforted by the child, or vice versa.

The other moment is the instrumental section from mm. 373–403. This music illustrates the "eating pantomime" where the soprano finally tastes green eggs and ham. Props may be used, or the entire section may be pantomimed imaginatively.

Regarding the props that are suggested, I have used two chairs to center the action, (although the performers do not remain in them throughout the piece), a backpack with "stuff" in it for Sam to use, funny glasses for the soprano, a boa for the blues section, and whatever is necessary for the eating pantomime. Stand lights are necessary for the "in the dark" section. In general, be creative and enjoy yourselves.

—ROBERT KAPILOW

duration: ca. 18 minutes

recording: Koch International Classics, 3–8900–2 H1
Angelina Réaux, soprano, Brett Tabisel, boy soprano, Robert Kapilow, piano,
and the New Jersey Chamber Music Society

Commissioned by the New Jersey Chamber Music Society

Premiere performance: December 11, 1993,
the New Jersey Chamber Music Society

Green Eggs and Ham is available in two other versions:

Chamber Ensemble [Fl (Picc), 2 Cl, Bn, Tpt, Hn, Perc(1), Pf, Cb] Score 50482454
Full Orchestra [2222 2220 Perc(2) Pf Strings] Score 50482506

Performance material is available on rental from the publisher.

GREEN EGGS AND HAM

Dr. Seuss

Robert Kapilow

With intensity

*When no rhythm is specified, speak in a normal pattern.

97

would not like them here or there. ____ I would not like them an - y - where.

100

I do not like green eggs and ham. I do not like them, Sam - I - am.

103

105

do not like them in a house. I do not like them with a mouse. I do not like them here or there. I

do not like them an-y-where. I do not like green eggs and ham. I do not like them

Sam-I-am.

Lightly

Sam:

135 Would you eat them in a box?

Sam:

140 Would you eat them with a fox?

146

151

Sop.: *f*   *p*

Not   in   a

226

I do not like green eggs

229

and ham. I do not like them Sam

232

I am.

Furioso

235

287
I do not like them, Sam, you see.

290
Not in a house. Not in a box. Not with a mouse.

293
cresc. poco a poco

Not with a fox. I will not eat them here or there. I do not

cresc. poco a poco

297
like them an - y - an - y - where!

**Slow,
astonished**

Funereal ♩ = ca. 44

Sam: You do not
like green
eggs and ham?

Sop.:
I do not
like them
Sam-I-am.

rit.

♩. = ca. 66

Sam:

Could you, would you,

with a goat?

Poco più mosso

Eating Pantomime

429

in a house. And I will eat them with a mouse.

432 *cresc.* **Sop. alone:**

And I will eat them here and there. Say! I will eat them

436

AN - Y - - WHERE! I

439

do so like green eggs and ham!